Mom

A Record Book For You

PUBLISHING

©1997 Havoc Publishing

ISBN 1-57977-106-8

Published and created by Havoc Publishing

San Diego, California

First Printing, May 1997

Designed by Juddesign

Cover illustration by Tori Larrick

Some images © 1997 PhotoDisc, Inc.

Printed in China

Please write to us for more information on our
Havoc Publishing Record Books and Products.

HAVOC PUBLISHING

7868 Silverton Avenue, Suite A

San Diego, California 92126

Mom

A Record Book For You

To

Rob, Jodi, Roey, and Madden

With all my love

Mom and Granny

Contents

All About Me

Our Family Tree

Family History

Photographs

Memorable Stories . . .

The Early Days

When I Was Growing Up

How the World Was . . .

School Days

My Best Friends

Photographs

The Times in Which I Lived

Inventions, People & Firsts . . .

My Favorite Things

Mom-isms

Some More Things . . .

Photographs

About My Parents

Contents

Their Marriage

About Your Father

The Proposal

Photographs

When You Were Born

My Favorite Traits About You

Stories About You . . .

On The Table

Favorite Times in The Kitchen

My Best Recipes

From My Garden

Keepsakes & Jewelry

Family Heirlooms

Photographs

Family Celebrations

Events & Traditions

Places I've Traveled

What I Wish For You

All About Me

My maiden name _Hochberg_

Who I was named after _Morris Airowitz_

My birth date _December 28, 1937_

My birth place _Brooklyn Women's Hospital Eastern Parkway, Brooklyn_

Growing up

_____

_____

_____

_____

Photo

Mom's pic

Our Family Tree

Great Grandmother

Great Grandfather

Great Grandfather

Great Grandmother

Grandmother

Sarah (Feldman) Ainowitz

Grandfather

Morris Ainowitz

Mother

Rebecca (Eva) Hochberg

Great Grandfather

Great Grandmother

Great Grandmother

Great Grandfather

Grandmother

Leah

Grandfather

Benjamin Hochberg

Father

Mordecai (Moy) Hochberg

Family History

Nationality of my family Parents born and raised in Brooklyn. Their parents born in Minsk and Pinsk, Russia

Different occupations My dad was a piece goods buyer and vice-president for Perlberg Originals - a gown company. Mom was always a stay-at-home mom.

Some interesting facts Mom as a teenager worked as a chicken plucker in her dad's poultry store. Quit school to help them in store.

Funny family tales handed down

Family Crest

Photograph

Photograph

Memorable Stories About Our Family

_____

_____

_____

_____

_____

_____

_____

_____

_____

The Early Days

My earliest memories

_____

_____

_____

_____

What my personality was like

_____

_____

_____

_____

What I looked like when I was young

_____

_____

_____

When I Was Growing Up

The cities I've lived in _Brooklyn - Greene Avenue, Saratoga Avenue; Bronx 2327 Valentine Avenue; Queens 136 Street and then 68 Drive and then 168 Street._

My favorite place to live _was in the Bronx - ages 9-12. Lots of friends and dad always took me to Yankee Stadium and the Polo Grounds_

CHORES

Who I've lived with

Mom, Dad, Carol and Eileen.
For a short while I lived w/ Aunt Frieda (mom's sister and Leah and Benjamin Hochberg)

Who was President *Franklin Delano Roosevelt*

Harry S. Truman

Famous scandals

Important hot issues at the time

Local issues

National issues *Pearl Harbor*

Attack

International issues *World*

War II

How The World Was

When I Was Young

Famous movie stars Farley Granger, Van Johnson, Peter Lawford, John Dereck, Tony Curtis

Favorite radio shows Baby Snooks - Fanny Brice, The Shadow

Famous musicians

What we danced to Love Is a Many Splendid Thing

Favorite television shows Milton Berle, I Love Lucy, Miss America, Jackie Gleason, Ed Sullivan

School Days

Where I went to school P.S. 115 - Bronx
P.S 117 - Queens

School pic here

Where I went to high school Forest Hills H.S.

What year I graduated 1955

Where I went to college Brooklyn College
New York University
Stonybrook University

School pic here

What year I graduated 1957, 1960, 1972

Funniest school story Having to sew my
8th grade graduation dress
in order to graduate.
I had to hurrip it so many
times that by the time I wore it
on graduation day it was literally
tearing apart at the seams.
the fabric was organza and does not
hold up to wear.

My favorite subject

Shorthand and
Typewriting

My not so favorite subject

Math

My favorite teacher was my

French teacher in

h.s. -- Mrs. Greenberg

My not so favorite teacher

my 3rd grade teacher

Mrs. Fishman

My Best Friends

My earliest friends Roz Pairess, Sandy Pairess, Carol Wolinsky, Sandy Wicker, Harriet Woixsky, Myrna Shuman

My friends now All of the above and Harriet Belkin, Arlene Schwartz Carol Haymes, Sydelle Stadler, etc.

How long I've known them Since high school and 1965 (meeting at Temple Beth Sholom, Smithlawn, NY)

How we met School, Temple, and many others while in college e.g. Rita Zuccala and Miriam Lefcourt

Stories about our friendship

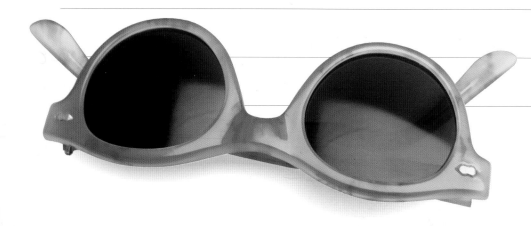

Photograph

The Times In Which I Lived

Clothes we wore

_____

_____

_____

What we did for entertainment and fun

_____

_____

_____

_____

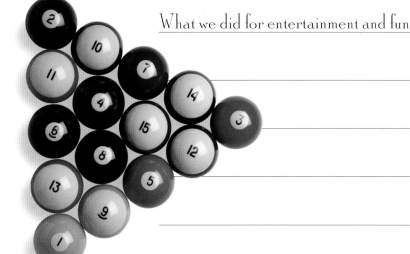

Inventions during my lifetime
_____
_____
_____
_____
_____
_____

Inventions,

People &

Famous people who made a difference
_____
_____
_____
_____
_____
_____

My first car

_____

_____

_____

My first plane trip

_____

_____

_____

Firsts In

My Life

Firsts I've experienced

_____

_____

_____

_____

_____

_____

_____

My Favorite Things

Color _____

Perfume _____

Season _____

Coffee _____

Person _____

Music _____

Poem _____

Book _____

Writer _____

Flower _____

Favorite outdoor activities _____
_____
_____
_____
_____
_____

Favorite ways to relax _____
_____
_____
_____
_____

Mom-isms

Things I've always said to you

_____

_____

_____

_____

Get up or you'll be late

Things I said that you hated

_____

_____

_____

_____

Eat your vegetables

Go brush your teeth

Some more things I want to tell you...

My values _____
_____
_____
_____

My passions _____
_____
_____
_____

My talents _____
_____
_____
_____

My hopes and dreams _____
_____
_____
_____

Photograph

Photograph

About My Parents

About my father _____

_____

_____

_____

_____

_____

About my mother _____

_____

_____

_____

_____

_____

_____

Their Marriage

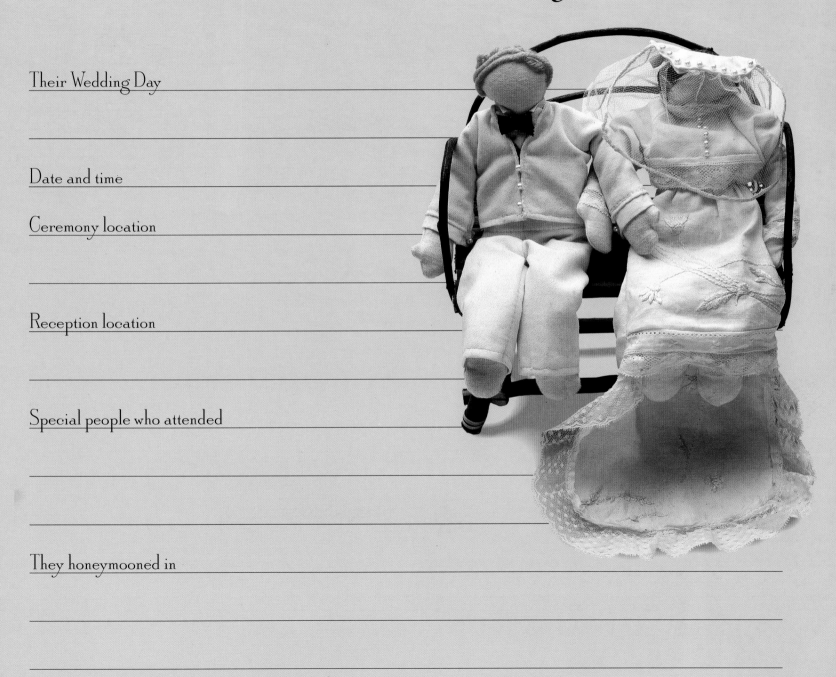

Their Wedding Day
_____

_____

Date and time
_____

Ceremony location
_____

_____

Reception location
_____

_____

Special people who attended
_____

_____

_____

They honeymooned in
_____

_____

_____

My hero!

Photo

About Your Father

His family
_____

_____

Where they are from
_____

_____

How we met
_____

_____

What attracted us to each other
_____

_____

_____

How he made his living
_____

_____

What a magician!

Photo

Cool dad!

Photo

My knight in shining armor!

Photo

The Proposal

Date _____

Place _____

How he proposed _____

_____

_____

_____

_____

_____

_____

_____

_____

Groom   Bride

Photo

About our wedding day

Date and time

Ceremony location

Reception location

Special people who participated in the wedding

We honeymooned in

Photo

Photograph

Photograph

When You Were Born

We are pleased to announce the birth of our child

Your birth date _____

Your birth place _____

Your full name _____

What it means _____

Who you were named after _____

What I was doing when I went into labor _____

_____

_____

I was in labor with you for _____

_____

_____

My Favorite Traits About You

Traits you received from me _____

_____

From your father _____

_____

From your grandparents _____

_____

Who you resemble the most _____

_____

Who your personality is the closest to _____

_____

_____

_____

Stories About When You Were Growing Up

_____

_____

_____

_____

_____

_____

_____

_____

1ST PLACE

Candid photo

Candid photo

On The Table

My favorite foods
_____
_____
_____

My least favorite foods
_____
_____

My favorite thing about meal time
_____
_____

Funniest food story
_____
_____

What I most like to cook
_____
_____
_____

What I least like to cook
_____
_____

What special things I did to prepare my finicky eater's meals

_____

_____

_____

_____

Favorite take-out foods

_____

_____

How often we ordered in

_____

_____

Favorite Kitchen Times

Who ate the cookie dough, and other tales

_____

_____

_____

_____

_____

Teaching you to cook

_____

_____

_____

What you liked to cook the most

What you liked to cook the least

My Best

Recipes

From My Garden

Keepsakes & Jewelry

_____

_____

_____

_____

_____

_____

_____

_____

_____

Family Heirlooms

Photograph

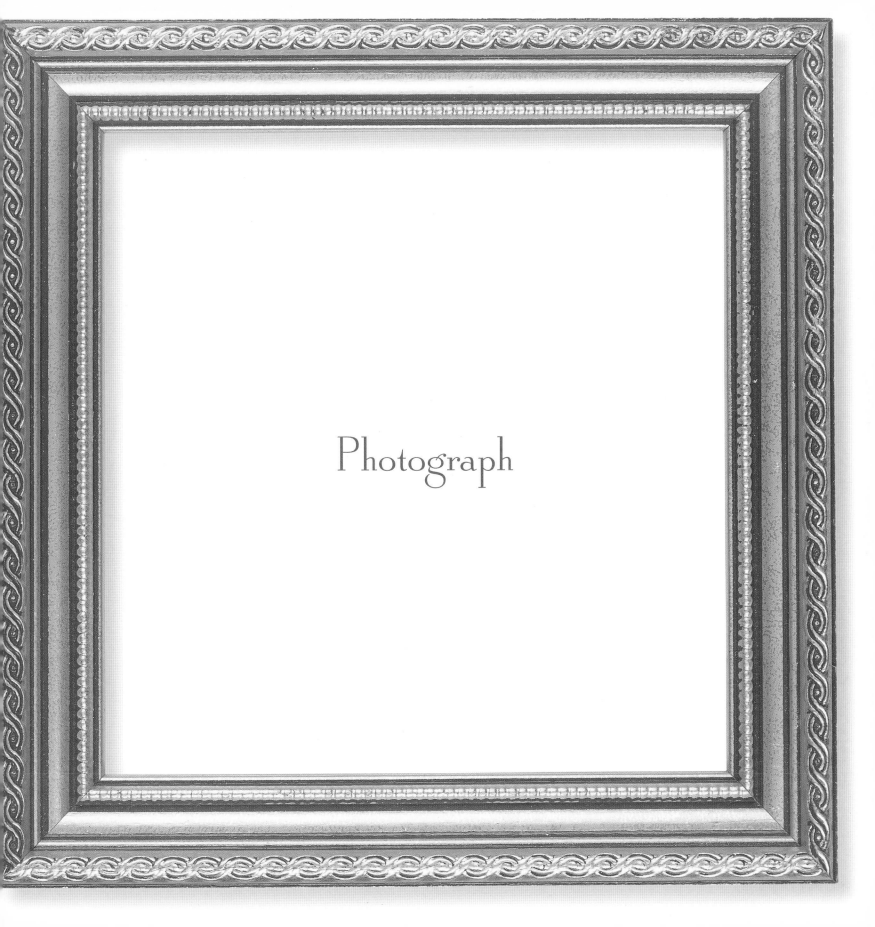

Family Celebrations,

Favorite things we celebrate

Special events

Most memorable family vacation

Events & Traditions

Special traditions

_____

_____

_____

_____

The holidays we celebrate

_____

_____

_____

_____

_____

Places I've Traveled

Different places I've been
_____

_____

_____

My favorite place
_____

The most exotic place I've been
_____

My most exciting trip
_____

_____

My most boring trip
_____

_____

My most memorable trip
_____

_____

What I Wish For You

Available Record Books
from Havoc

Animal Antics - Cats

Animal Antics - Dogs

Couples

Girlfriends

Golf

Grandmother

Our Honeymoon

Mom

Sisters

Tying the Knot

Traveling Adventures

Please write to us with your ideas for additional
Havoc Publishing Record Books and Products

HAVOC PUBLISHING

7868 Silverton Avenue, Suite A

San Diego, California 92126